QUESTIONS AND ANSWERS ABOUT
PLANET EARTH

Contents

Seasons and Climate

The Earth not only orbits the Sun, but also rotates on its own axis as it does so. The Earth's axis is in fact tilted—meaning that neither of the Earth's poles faces the Sun directly. This tilted axis is responsible for weather and different climates.

Quick Q's:

1. What causes day and night?

The Earth turning on its axis is responsible for day and night. At any time, half the Earth faces the Sun, where it is day, and half faces away, where it is night.

2. Does the Sun really rise in the east?

The Earth spins in an eastward direction. This makes the Sun appear as if it is rising in the east and setting in the west.

3. Why are days longer in summer and shorter in winter?

The angle at which sunlight falls on a particular area determines the length of day and night in that region. During summer the Sun stays above the horizon longer, making the days longer.

4. What is the Coriolis effect?

The wind moves to the right in the northern hemisphere and to the left in the southern hemisphere. This is called the Coriolis effect. It is caused by the Earth's rotation. It is mainly responsible for thunderstorms and hurricanes.

Q How is weather different from climate?

A Sunlight falls at varying angles onto the Earth's surface, heating up each of its regions differently. The difference in temperature eventually leads to different types of weather. A climate is when particular weather conditions prevail in a place for an extended period of time. So we can talk about the weather tomorrow or this month, but when we talk of climate we are talking of much longer time periods—decades or even centuries.

Q What is a season?

A A season is a period within a year defined by distinct weather. The tilt in the Earth's axis is responsible for seasons. In temperate and polar regions four seasons are recognized—spring, summer, fall, and winter. Some tropical and subtropical regions have a rainy season (sometimes called a monsoon season) and a dry season, while others have hot, rainy, and cool seasons.

Q What are the factors that influence weather on the Earth?

A Temperature, rainfall, wind, cloud and atmospheric pressure are the main factors that influence weather patterns across the world. Wind is caused by the unequal heating of the Earth's surface. When the air above a certain region becomes warm and light, it rises and heavier, cooler air sweeps across from another area to take its place. This movement of air is called wind. Atmospheric pressure also affects the movement of wind, which always flows from a region of high pressure to that of low pressure. The difference in pressure between the two areas determines the speed with which the wind blows. If there is a small difference, we feel a breeze. If the difference is large, it leads to a storm. If the wind is flowing over a large water body such as a sea, it can pick up moisture and carry clouds and rain with it. Low pressure usually means stormy weather and rain, while high pressure usually means lots of sun and not much wind. There are other factors, such as the ocean currents created by the Earth's rotation, which also influence weather.

▼ **The blowing wind**
The wind always blows from an area of high pressure to an area of low pressure.

Q How are clouds formed?

A The Sun's heat causes water in the oceans, rivers and lakes to evaporate and form water vapor. The warm water vapor rises upward, and as it rises, it cools down. As a result, the water vapor in the air condenses to form clouds containing tiny droplets of water. These droplets grow larger in size and finally fall down as rain. Sometimes, the temperature is so low that these droplets freeze into ice crystals and fall down as snow.

The water cycle
All the water in the Earth's atmosphere, both on its surface and underground, is a part of the water cycle. The water is recycled again and again.

Water stored in ice and snow
Snow melts down to streams
Precipitation
Water stored in the atmosphere
Condensation
Transpiration
Evaporation
Water stored in oceans

Q Which is the place on the Earth that has the coldest climate?

A The climate of Antarctica is the coldest on Earth. Nearly all of Antarctica is covered with an ice sheet about 2.5 kilometers thick. The lowest temperature recorded on this continent is -89.6 °C (-128.56 °F) at Vostok research station at the center of the East Antarctic Ice Sheet.

▲ **Cold places**
The closer you are to the North or South Pole, the colder it is. Some animals have adapted so they can survive in the freezing temperatures.

Solstices and equinoxes

In the northern hemisphere the longest day falls during the summer, on 21 June, when the northern half of the Earth is tipped toward the Sun. This is known as the summer solstice. In the extreme north the Sun does not set at all during this period. During the winter solstice (22 December), the northern part of the Earth is tipped away from the Sun, resulting in the longest night of the year. On 23 September and 21 March the Earth is positioned in such a way that the length of day and night is equal (12 hours each). These days are known as the autumnal and spring equinoxes respectively.

Mountains, Valleys, and Caves

Mountains are formed when two of the continental plates that make up the Earth's crust collide. The force caused by the collision pushes both plates (also called tectonic plates) upward, creating a mountain. Valleys and caves are also natural features created by erosion and the movement of the Earth's crust.

▲ **Climbing mountains**
Scientists climb mountains to study them.

Quick Q's:

1. Which is the highest mountain peak in the world?

At a height of about 8,848 meters (29,028 feet) above sea level, Mount Everest is the highest peak in the world. It is a part of the Himalayan mountain range that was formed about 10–15 million years ago.

2. How big is the Grand Canyon?

The Grand Canyon is about 446 kilometers (277 miles) long and roughly 1.6 kilometers (1 mile) deep. It is made up of several layers of rock, each one older than the one above it.

3. How are glacial valleys formed?

When glaciers slowly flow downhill, they collect many pieces of rock on the way. These pieces scrape against the valley floor, digging deeper into it, until a U-shaped valley is formed.

Q Can we live on mountains?

A It is not easy to live on high mountains. The weather is extremely cold and not suitable for farming. At very high altitudes, oxygen levels are so low that it becomes difficult to breathe without an oxygen tank and mask.

Q How are mountains different from plateaus?

A Like a mountain, a plateau is higher than its surrounding area. However, plateaus have a flat top, while mountains have peaks. Like mountains, plateaus are formed when two continental plates collide, but erosion due to wind and water flattens the top. Plateaus are not as tall as mountains. In fact, some plateaus, such as the Tibetan Plateau, lie between two mountain ranges.

Q How is a valley formed?

A A valley is a low-lying area of land that is usually found at the foot of mountains or hills. The most common way valleys are formed is by the erosion of land from running water. River valleys are formed by the action of the river. As a river flows downhill, it cuts through the land like a knife. Over thousands of years the river erodes the land to form a valley, usually in the shape of a V. In contrast, valleys formed by glaciers are often U-shaped, because they are formed by rocks carried in the glacier that erode the soil.

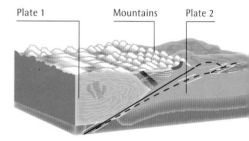

Plate 1   Mountains   Plate 2

▲ **Forming a mountain**
Mountains are formed when two of the Earth's tectonic plates collide. The crust is forced up between the two plates, giving birth to the mountain range.

◀ **U-shaped valley**
Glaciers carry stones that scour out the soil, forming U-shaped valleys. Rivers, in contrast, usually form V-shaped valleys.

Q What is a canyon?

A A deep valley with cliffs on both sides is called a canyon. Sometimes a large river may run through a canyon. The Grand Canyon in Arizona, USA is the world's largest canyon. It was formed by the Colorado River. Million of years ago, this region was covered by sea. Slowly, a part of the sea floor was pushed up to form a plateau. Over the years, rainwater collected to form a river. This river cut into the rocks on the plateau to form the canyon

Caves of lava

When volcanoes erupt, lava flows down the side of the volcano. The surface of the lava cools and becomes solid, while hot lava continues to flow underneath it. Once the eruption is over, there is a hollow tube, or cave, left behind underneath the hard crust of lava.

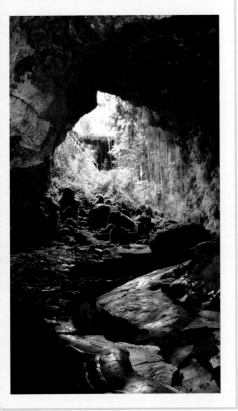

Q What are caves?

A Caves are huge holes under the ground, in cliffs or under the sea. Caves can be formed in many ways. Most rock caves, especially limestone caves, are formed by rainwater that seeps into tiny cracks in the rocks. The rainwater contains minerals and chemicals that slowly causes the rock to dissolve, leaving behind a large hole. This process may take several thousand, or even a few million years.

Q How are sea caves formed?

A Sea caves are formed by waves that wear away the rocks at the base of a cliff. These rocks are usually very weak and have tiny cracks in them. The continuous pounding of the waves causes the tiny cracks to widen and soon the rocks begin to crumble and form small hollows. These hollows keep expanding as sand, gravel and rocks brought by the waves erode their inner walls. Some sea caves are submerged during high tide and can only be seen when the water goes down at low tide.

▲ **Sea cave**
Sea caves are most common in areas where the rocks on the coast are soft.

Q What is a rift valley?

A A rift valley is created when two tectonic plates pull away from each other, leaving a low space in the middle. The Great Rift Valley is the best known rift valley in the world. It covers a distance of over 6,000 kilometers (3,700 miles), stretching from northern Syria in West Asia to central Mozambique in East Africa. It began to form about 35 million years ago, when the African and Arabian tectonic plates began to pull apart. Even today it is still growing, as East Africa slowly separates from the rest of Africa.

▼ **Rift in the Earth**
When two of the Earth's plates move away from each other, the soil covering them falls down and forms a rift valley. The rift valleys in East Africa now form a series of lakes.

Normal Faults

Earth's Crust

Mantle

Other Landforms

Rivers, lakes, and streams are natural bodies of water that are found across the world. When it rains or when snow on mountains melts, the water flows down the slopes, forming streams. Several streams join together to form a river. Small rivers drain into larger rivers. The water in rivers keeps flowing until it reaches the sea, though a few rivers hit very dry desert land and dry up.

Quick Q's:

1. Which is the largest freshwater lake in the world?

Lake Superior, one of the Great Lakes of North America, is the largest freshwater lake in the world. This lake is over 560 kilometers (350 miles) long and about 257 kilometers (160 miles) wide.

2. What is the Sahara known for?

The Sahara is the largest hot desert in the world. Located in Africa, it spreads across Mauritania, Morocco, Mali, Algeria, Tunisia, Niger, Libya, Chad, Egypt, Sudan and Eritrea.

3. Which is the longest river?

The Nile is the longest river on Earth. It flows for 6,695 kilometers (4,184 miles).

4. Why is Lake Baikal special?

Lake Baikal in southern Siberia is the deepest lake in the world, with a maximum depth of 1,637 meters (5,371 feet). It has been around for almost 30 million years.

▲ **Largest freshwater lake**
Lake Superior in North America is the largest freshwater lake in the world by area and the third largest by volume.

Q How are lakes formed?

A Sometimes, rainwater collects in big hollows in the ground to form lakes. These hollows can be formed by the movement of the plates that make up the Earth's crust, or by moving glaciers. Lakes are also formed by landslides that leave huge depressions in the ground. Most lakes and rivers contain freshwater. In places containing a large amount of salt, lake water can be salty.

◀ **View from space**
This photograph, taken from an artificial satellite, shows Lake Baikal in southern Siberia. The size of the lake has been reduced in recent years, as more and more of its water is taken away for irrigation. It is considered to be one of the most serious problems in the region.

Q What are waterfalls?

A Sometimes the surface over which a river flows drops suddenly. Then the water flows over to form a waterfall. There are different kinds of waterfalls. A cascade waterfall flows down a series of natural rock steps. There are no steps in a free-falling waterfall. In a fan waterfall, the water spreads out as it falls down. Angel Falls in Venezuela is the highest free-falling waterfall in the world. The water falls 807 meters (2,648 feet) without any interruption. Often, the sunlight falling over a waterfall creates a rainbow.

Q Do rivers flood?

A Yes, they do. Rivers often overflow their banks and flood the land around them. This can happen when there has been a lot of rain or a lot of snow has melted in the mountain where the river starts its journey. Floods are often very destructive. They can damage crops and houses and kill people. But in the long run they can also do some good. They bring fresh soil down the river and spread it on the flooded land. Egyptian farmers have been dependent on the annual flooding of the Nile for thousands of years. The Amazon and the Ganges rivers regularly bring fertile soil to the agricultural areas downstream.

▼ **Longest river**
The ancient civilization of Egypt started along the banks of the Nile.

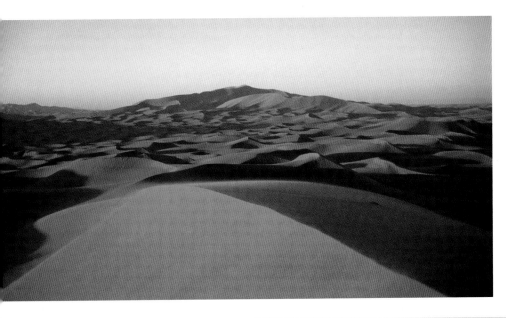

◄ Largest desert
The Sahara is the world's largest hot desert. It spreads right across northern Africa from the Atlantic Ocean in the west to the Red Sea in the east. Sand and rock cover most of the dry Sahara, but there are oases where people have lived for centuries.

What is a desert?

A desert is a dry region with very little rainfall. During the day, temperatures can rise above 50 °C (122 °F). However, nights in a desert can be extremely cold. Most deserts are covered with sand and rocks. Animals and plants that live in this habitat are specially adapted to life with little water and extreme changes in temperature.

What are montane deserts?

Some deserts, located at very high altitudes, are known as montane deserts. They are common in the Himalayas. Some, like the Tibetan Plateau, are relatively flat. Very few animals can survive the extreme cold and dryness, but the yak lives in Tibet.

What is an oasis?

For most part deserts are dry and have no water bodies. However, small springs with trees and plants growing around them can be found in certain places. These isolated regions are called oases. An oasis is vital for all forms of life in the desert.

Cold desert

Most deserts are hot during the day, but some deserts are in the coldest parts of the Earth. Some cold deserts are covered in ice throughout the year, allowing very few plants to grow. Cold deserts are also not very suitable for animals. Few species can survive such extreme cold for long periods of time. Antarctica is the largest cold desert in the world. Patagonia in the southernmost part of South America and Gobi in Mongolia are also cold deserts.

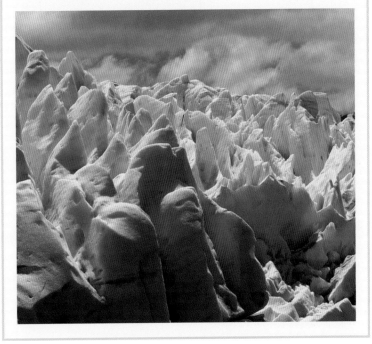

Oceans

Oceans occupy about 70 percent of the Earth's surface. There are five oceans in the world. They are the Atlantic, Pacific, Indian, Arctic, and Antarctic oceans. The surface under the oceans is called the ocean floor. Like land, the ocean floor also has natural features like plains, valleys, and mountains.

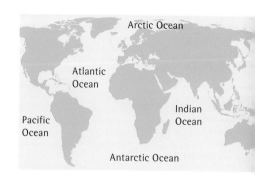

▲ **Oceans of the world**
The five oceans of the world cover over 70 percent of the surface of the Earth.

Quick Q's:

1. Which is the largest of all oceans?

The Pacific Ocean is the world's largest and deepest ocean. It has an average depth of over 4,000 meters (13,100 feet). It has the world's deepest trench —the Mariana Trench near Japan. The Challenger Deep in the Mariana Trench is the deepest point on Earth —about 11,033 meters (36,200 feet) deep.

2. What causes an ocean current?

An ocean current is a mass of water that keeps moving in one direction. Surface currents are caused by wind and the Earth's rotation. Underwater currents are the result of differences in temperature and salt content of the water.

3. What is a black smoker?

When water seeps into the crust of the ocean floor through cracks, it may be heated by the magma below. As pressure builds up within the crust, the hot water shoots up through these cracks. These jets of warm water are often black due to their mineral content, so they are called black smokers.

Q **Which ocean is also known as the Southern Ocean?**

A The Antarctic Ocean is also called the Southern Ocean. Until recently, the Antarctic Ocean was considered to be a part of the other main oceans, as it was actually formed from parts of the Pacific, Atlantic, and Indian oceans. In the year 2000, however, it was officially named the "Southern Ocean."

Q **What is the ocean floor like?**

A The ocean floor is far from flat. The edges of islands and continents gently slope into the surrounding water to form an area called a continental shelf that is higher than rest of the ocean floor. A continental shelf usually extends about 75 kilometers (47 miles) out to sea but some, like the Siberian shelf in the Arctic Ocean, can extend up to 1,500 kilometers (932 miles). The continental shelf contains large deposits of petroleum, natural gas and minerals. It also receives the most sunlight, so marine life thrives here. The point where the continental shelf starts to plunge steeply toward the deep ocean floor is called the continental slope. It is here that the deep canyons of the ocean are found.

▲ **Not a flat floor**
The ocean floor has mountains and valleys. Some of the mountains are tall enough to rise above the surface and form islands.

Q **What causes the formation of mountains and valleys on the ocean floor?**

A Like the rest of the Earth, the ocean floor is divided into tectonic plates. The movement of these plates is responsible for features like ridges, trenches, and valleys. Ridges are formed when two plates drift apart. Boiling rock from inside the Earth, called magma, oozes out through the cracks between the plates and cools to form a ridge. Trenches are formed when a heavier plate sinks down under a lighter one.

◀ **Ocean currents**
The water in the oceans and seas is always in motion, due to the rotation of the Earth, the gravitational pull of the Sun and Moon, and the difference in temperature and salt content of the water. These movements form strong currents in the oceans, both at the surface and deep down.

Q What is a mid-ocean ridge?

A The ridges on the ocean floor are connected to form a single chain called a mid-ocean ridge. The mid-ocean ridge is over 80,000 kilometers (50,000 miles) long and is the longest mountain chain on Earth. On average, these mountains lie about 2,500 meters (8,200 feet) below the ocean surface, with their peaks sometimes breaking above.

North American Plate — Eurasian Plate — Iceland — Mid-Atlantic Ridge — Atlantic Ocean

◀ **Mountains down there**
The mid-ocean ridge exists on the floor of all the oceans in the world. The diagram shows a part of the mid-Atlantic ridge, which extends below Iceland. Many volcanoes lie along the ridge.

Q How are volcanic islands formed?

A Volcanoes under the sea are responsible for the formation of volcanic islands. As magma keeps oozing out of a volcano, it can collect, causing the volcano to grow and rise above the ocean surface as an island.

Q What is special about the Hawaiian group of islands?

A Volcanic activity does not always take place near plate boundaries. There are some places deep inside the Earth that are much hotter than others. As a result, there is constant volcanic activity above these spots, known as hot spots. This activity leads to the formation of underwater volcanoes. The constant movement of tectonic plates eventually shifts the volcano away from the hot spot. Soon, another volcano is created in the area near the hot spot. This often leads to the formation of a chain of islands, such as the Hawaiian Islands.

Q How are waves different from tides?

A Waves are caused by wind, while tides are the regular rise and fall of the ocean's surface caused by the gravitational pull of the Sun and the Moon on the water that is in the ocean. Waves are formed when winds blow over the surface of the ocean. Stronger winds create larger waves. The water in a wave normally moves in circles. As a wave approaches the land it is slowed down by the rising slope of the seabed. But it is the bottom portion of the wave that is slowed down. The top part of the wave keeps moving and crashes on to the shore as a breaker.

▼ **The breaker**
Breakers are higher when the seabed slopes down quickly from the shore. The beaches of Hawaii and Australia are famous for their high breakers.

Beach — Surf — Deep water

Feeling the heat

The temperature of the water from an underwater hot spring can be as high as 400 °C (752 °F). However, this water is rich in minerals, helping some unusual creatures like giant tubeworms and eyeless shrimps survive in an environment where nothing else can live.

Volcanoes

A volcano is a mountain through which molten rock and gases erupt from the Earth's crust. Volcanoes are named after the Roman god of fire, Vulcan.

▲ **Volcanic rocks**
Hardened lava from volcanoes forms new rocks.

Quick Q's:

1. Which is the highest volcano on Earth?

Mauna Loa in Hawaii is the highest volcano on Earth. It rises about 4 kilometers above sea level; below that, it extends to 5 kilometers down before it reaches the seabed. Its massive weight has pushed the volcano down a further 8 kilometers below the seabed! So Mauna Loa is 17 kilometers (56,000 feet) from its base to its summit.

2. Which is the most active volcano?

Mount St Helens in Washington State of USA is the most active volcano. It last erupted in 1980.

3. What are geysers?

Geysers are jets of hot water that erupt from the Earth. When water trickles down into the hot molten rock under the Earth's crust, it is heated up. As the water becomes hotter, the pressure builds up, finally causing it to spurt out.

Q **How are volcanoes formed?**

A Volcanoes are formed by tectonic plates colliding with each other. The heavier plate is usually forced down below the lighter one, where part of it is melted by the heat of the crash. The melting plate forms magma or molten rock that collects below the surface of the Earth in magma chambers. As the amount of magma increases, the pressure inside the chamber rises. This creates a mountain, or volcano. The volcano has a cone, from which gases and lava may trickle out. When the pressure gets too high, the whole chamber explodes, ejecting the magma. This is a volcanic eruption.

▲ **Movements of the Earth**
The tectonic plates that cover the Earth can move in various ways, and are constantly rubbing against one another, sometimes violently.

Q **What are the various things that happen during a volcanic eruption?**

A Magma, or molten rock, erupts through the surface of Earth during an eruption. Magma that comes out is called lava. It can be thick and slow moving or thin and fast. Pieces of rock and ash also erupt from the volcano. Pumice stone, a light rock full of air bubbles, is formed in an explosive volcanic eruption. These volcanic materials are called pyroclasts.

▲ **Hot water**
Old Faithful is a geyser of hot water in the Yellowstone National Park, USA. It erupts from the Earth every 90 minutes, on average.

Q **Do volcanoes erupt regularly?**

A Volcanoes may be active, intermittent, dormant or extinct depending on how often they erupt. Active volcanoes erupt often. Intermittent volcanoes erupt at regular intervals. Dormant volcanoes have been inactive for a long time. They are the most dangerous because they are merely "sleeping" and can erupt without warning. Extinct volcanoes have not erupted for thousands of years. It is difficult to distinguish between dormant and extinct volcanoes because some volcanoes may remain quiet for a long time before suddenly becoming active again.

▼ **Active volcano**
Kilauea, in Hawaii, is considered the most active volcano in the world. It last erupted in 1983.

Q What are the different types of volcanoes on the Earth?

A Volcanoes are classified according to their shapes and the type of material they are composed of. A shield volcano is a gentle sloping volcano that has long-lasting, gentle eruptions. Most of the volcanoes in the Hawaiian islands are shield volcanoes. A strato volcano is a steep volcano shaped like a cone. When it erupts, it emits gases, ash, pumice, and lava. These volcanic eruptions are accompanied by deadly mudflows, making strato volcanoes the most dangerous among the volcanoes on Earth. Famous strato volcanoes include Mount Vesuvius in Italy and Mount Fuji in Japan.

The cone shape
The cone-shaped volcano, known as a strato volcano, may be the most famous, but is only one of many types of volcano.

Q Are there volcanoes under the sea?

A Volcanoes form under the sea in the same way as on land. When two oceanic plates collide, one may get pushed under the other. The heat generated by the crash causes one plate to melt and form magma. The hot magma rises and forms an underwater volcano, just as it does on land. The Vailulu volcano in Ta'u Island in the Pacific Ocean is an underwater volcano.

Ring of Fire

◄ Ring of fire
The ring of fire around the Pacific Ocean has been responsible for some of the most destructive volcanic eruptions and earthquakes in human history, including the 1906 San Francisco earthquake and the 1995 earthquake in Kobe, Japan. The biggest earthquake ever recorded was also in the ring of fire—the Great Chilean earthquake of 1960, 9.5 on the Richter scale.

Q· What is the "ring of fire"?

A The area encircling the Pacific Ocean is called the ring of fire because most of the Earth's active volcanoes are located in a ring around it. The massive Pacific plate is expanding continuously at the edges of the ocean and hitting the other smaller plates next to it. The collisions cause frequent volcanic activity and earthquakes. The ring of fire stretches from New Zealand, along the eastern coastline of Asia and along the western coast of North and South America.

An island disappears

One of the largest volcanic eruptions recorded in recent history occurred on the island of Krakatau in Indonesia in 1883. The eruption was so massive that most of the island disappeared into the sea (pale blue area between the two small islands). Over much of the world, the sky was dark with ash for days.

Earthquakes and Tsunamis

The Earth is made up of a boiling hot, liquid center covered by a crust. This crust is broken into pieces called tectonic plates, which move around, sometimes colliding into each other. These collisions lead to earthquakes, some so small that they are hardly felt. But some earthquakes are so massive that they cause the ground to shake violently, destroying houses and killing people.

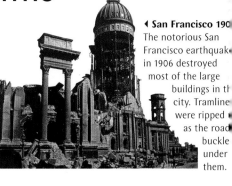

◀ San Francisco 190[
The notorious San Francisco earthquak[in 1906 destroyed most of the large buildings in th city. Tramline were ripped as the road buckle under them.

Quick Q's:

1. Which is the worst earthquake in history?

In 1556, an earthquake struck three provinces in China. About 830,000 people were killed in the disaster. It was the worst earthquake in history.

2. Can we predict earthquakes?

No, we cannot. The movements of the Earth are too complex for us to be able to predict earthquakes. But we do know the lines along which the Earth's plates meet, so we know the areas that are more likely to have earthquakes.

3. What is liquefaction?

Liquefaction is caused by the violent shaking of the ground during an earthquake. Moist soil or sand turns into slurry, like quicksand. This liquid can suck in entire buildings.

4. Is a tsunami the same as a tidal wave?

A tsunami is different from a tidal wave. A tidal wave is generated by high winds, but a tsunami is caused by underwater earthquakes, landslides or volcanic eruptions.

Q Do earthquakes occur everywhere?

A Earthquakes usually occur along a region called a fault, where broken rocks under the Earth's surface rub against each other and cause tremors. Faults are marked by cracks on the Earth's surface, caused by the movement of tectonic plates. Most faults are located near the edges of the plates, but small faults can be found far away from the boundaries.

Q How do faults produce earthquakes?

A Faults allow the rock fragments that form the Earth's crust to move about. Over a period of time, plate movement builds up pressure, causing rocks along a fault to bend or break with a jolt. This sudden movement releases energy that moves through the surface of the Earth in the form of waves. This is an earthquake. The energy moves out in a circle from the point where the movement occurs.

▶ **Fault in the Earth**
The San Andreas Fault in California, USA, is one of the few faults in the Earth's surface that can actually be seen by any observer on the ground. Most of the other faults are covered by soil or water. These faults mark the lines on the Earth's surface where two tectonic plates of the Earth meet. As a result, areas around these faults are the ones most prone to volcanic activity and earthquakes.

Q Where is an earthquake most dangerous

A The point inside the Earth where the rocks first begin to break is the focus of the earthquake. The point on the Earth's surface that lies directly above the focus is called the "epicenter." This is where the earthquake is strongest. In a major earthquake, the maximum damage takes place at the epicenter, and there is less damage as you get further away from it. The epicenter is directly above the hypocenter, the actual location of the energy released inside the Earth. Seismic waves ripple out from the hypocenter. After an earthquake, scientists can find the center by looking at the seismic wave data from three separate locations. The extent of the damage caused by an earthquake may also depend on the nature of the soil.

Q Do earthquakes occur only on land?

A Earthquakes also occur under the ocean. Sometimes, massive earthquakes that start on the ocean floor can create giant, destructive waves called tsunamis. These waves move at great speeds (up to about 800 kilometers or 500 miles per hour) and can travel thousands of kilometers across the ocean. In deep water, the waves are not very high. They gain strength and height as they approach the shore. Tsunamis can be about 30 meters (98 feet) high. These huge waves break on to the shore with a great deal of force, bringing down trees and large buildings.

When disaster strikes

On 26 December 2004, a tsunami spread across the Indian Ocean, killing over 250,000 people. The tsunami was caused by an underwater earthquake that occurred near the island of Sumatra, Indonesia. The tsunami hit the coasts of about 15 countries. Its effect was felt even in the southern tip of Africa, about 8,500 kilometers (5,300 miles) away from the epicenter of the earthquake!

Before

After

Q Do earthquakes cause destruction every time they occur?

A Some earthquakes are extremely destructive. A strong quake can topple buildings and bridges, trapping people underneath them. If gas pipes and electrical wires break, they can start fires that rage for several days. Earthquakes can also cause landslides and avalanches. The violent shaking of the Earth sometimes loosens chunks of snow or mud that slide down the slopes of mountains and hills, burying houses and people under them.

Q Can an earthquake be measured?

A Earthquakes are measured using the Richter scale. It was developed in 1935 by Charles Richter and Beno Gutenberg at the California Institute of Technology. This scale uses numbers from 1 to 10 to measure the intensity of an earthquake. Each increase of one point on the scale means a ten-fold increase in the strength of the earthquake. So a level 5.0 earthquake is ten times stronger than a level 4.0 earthquake. The Richter scale works by measuring vibrations around the epicenter of an earthquake.

▲ **Earthquake effect**
An earthquake can lead to a deadly avalanche or a landslide that can cause more damage than the original earthquake.

▲ **Old instrument**
The ancient Chinese invented an instrument that reacted to tremors in the Earth—a ball dropped from the mouth of the dragon into the mouth of a frog, warning people about a possible earthquake.

Hurricanes and Tornadoes

Sometimes the weather becomes wild. Blizzards, thunderstorms, hurricanes, and heatwaves are some examples of extreme weather conditions. Such severe weather often causes a great deal of damage to both life and property. Hurricanes and tornadoes especially are very destructive.

Quick Q's:

1. Can hurricane winds be measured?

Hurricanes are divided into five categories depending on their wind speeds. Category 5 hurricanes are the worst, causing maximum damage. Winds of a category 5 hurricane can reach speeds of about 250 kilometers per hour (155 miles per hour). Category 1 hurricanes are much weaker, and only travel at 119–153 kilometers per hour (74–95 miles per hour).

2. What is a storm surge?

Sometimes the strong winds of a hurricane can cause the water level in the ocean to rise. Huge waves hit the coast along with the storm, causing severe flooding. This is called a storm surge.

3. What is the Fujita scale?

The Fujita scale is used to measure the intensity of a tornado. It ranks tornadoes by the damage caused to man-made structures.

4. How did tornadoes get their name?

The word tornado is from the Spanish *tomear*, meaning "to turn."

Q What is a hurricane?

A Hurricanes are large, violent storms that form over the ocean near the equator. These storms are accompanied by winds that travel at an average speed of about 119 kilometers per hour (74 miles per hour). Hurricanes usually occur between June and November.

▲ **Eye of the hurricane**
This satellite image clearly shows the eye of the hurricane, an area of calm in the middle of the storm.

Q How does a hurricane form?

A When the air above the sea is heated it rises, creating an area of low pressure. Coole wind moves in to take place of the warm air. The Earth's rotation causes the rising hot air to twist and form a cylinder. As the warm air rises higher, it cools down and forms huge thunderclouds and finally becomes a hurricane. Meanwhile, the cooler air at the bottom also becomes warm, adding more energy to the storm.

Q What is the eye of a hurricane?

A The center of a hurricane is called the eye. The eye is an area of clear skies, light winds and no rain. It is also the warmest par of the storm and is surrounded by a wall of heavy rain and strong winds. People faced with a hurricane usually experience the heav rain and strong winds first, then there is a period of calm as the eye passes over the are followed by more stormy weather.

▼ **Huge destroyer**
In 2005, Hurricane Katrina, seen here in a satellite image, destroyed large parts of the city of New Orlear in the USA.

Q What is the worst hurricane on record?

A The hurricane that ripped through the Caribbean islands of Martinique, St. Eustatius and Barbados in October 1780 is the worst on record so far. It killed nearly 22,000 people. However, this hurricane does not have a name, because the practice of giving human names to major hurricanes started during World War II.

The making of a storm
Warm air rises from the sea, taking water with it in the form of a funnel, and starting a storm.

Q What is a tornado?

A A tornado is a black, funnel-shaped storm that is highly destructive. These storms usually form where cold polar winds mix with warm, moist tropical winds. They start as rotating thunderstorms called supercells. Gradually the spinning wind in the supercell forms the funnel of a tornado. The wind in the funnel spins so fast that it sucks objects into it like a vacuum cleaner.

Q What is Tornado Alley?

A Tornado Alley is an area that extends across the Great Plains of the USA, from central Texas in the south to the border of Canada in the north. The conditions in this region are most suitable for the formation of severe tornadoes, which occur during spring and early summer.

Chasing the storm

Most of us would prefer to stay as far away as possible from all violent storms, especially hurricanes and tornadoes. Some people however, chase hurricanes and tornadoes. For these people, confronting a storm is exciting. Storm chasers use special equipment to locate and follow storms. They usually have a well-equipped vehicle fitted with the latest technology, including cameras, radios, scanners, and first-aid kits. The videos, photographs and all other data collected by storm chasers have helped scientists understand hurricanes and tornadoes better.

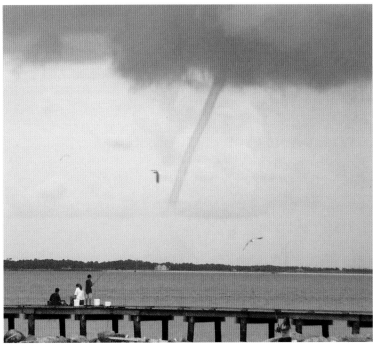

Q What is a waterspout?

A Tornadoes usually travel across land. However, occasionally, tornadoes pass over water. In these cases, the high-speed winds suck in water, creating tall columns of spinning water called waterspouts. These waterspouts are weaker than land tornadoes and occur in warm tropical oceans. However, they are still strong enough to cause huge damage to any boat or ship caught in them.

▲ **Waterspout**
When tornadoes pass over water, they suck the water up into tall spinning columns called waterspouts.

ARCTURUS

This edition published in 2011 by Arcturus Publishing Limited
26/27 Bickels Yard, 151-153 Bermondsey Street,
London SE1 3HA

ISBN: 978-1-84858-159-3
CH002009US
Supplier 15, Date 1011, Print run 1194

Designers: Q2A India and Jane Hawkins
Editors: Ella Fern, Fiona Tulloch and Alex Woolf

Printed in China